"I realize how fortunate I was to spend the first half of my life with a passion, thanks to my hockey career. It took me a while to realize it, but now I feel fortunate to have lived the second half of my life with a purpose."

– Travis Roy

TRAVIS ROY
QUADRIPLEGIA
and a
LIFE OF PURPOSE

DAVID H. HENDRICKSON
with a special foreword
by Travis Roy

Pentucket Publishing
www.pentucketpublishing.com

Travis Roy
Quadriplegia and a Life of Purpose

The three interviews reprinted in this book originally appeared on U.S. College Hockey Online (USCHO.com).

All proceeds from the sale of this book will be donated to the Travis Roy Foundation.

ISBN-13: 978-1-948134-01-9
ISBN-10: 1-948134-01-2

Table of Contents

To Travis
and all those affected by
spinal cord injuries

TRAVIS ROY
QUADRIPLEGIA
and a
LIFE OF PURPOSE

Introduction

O ver the years, I've written three feature stories about Travis Roy. In an alternate universe in which his spinal cord injury never happened, I might have still written three pieces about him, but they would been about his on-ice hockey exploits. Hockey East Rookie of the year, perhaps. Boston University hero of the Beanpot. Maybe even Hobey Baker Award winner as the top player in college hockey.

Instead, back here in the real world, the three stories have been about his injury just eleven seconds into his college hockey career, and his subsequent life as a quadriplegic. Written in 1997, 1999, and 2015, they're collected here for the first time, along with all-new introductions and a foreword by Travis himself.

All proceeds will be donated to the Travis Roy Foundation, which allocates grants to spinal cord injury survivors and funds research into a cure.

* * *

Travis's injury came a year before U.S. College Hockey Online (USCHO.com) began operations, so instead of sitting in a press box, I was watching the game on TV. When Travis went down after crashing headfirst into the boards, then didn't get up, I immediately felt the chill of fear.

Seventeen years earlier, I'd watched Oakland Raiders defensive back Jack Tatum deliver a crushing blow to New England Patriots wide receiver Darryl Stingley, one which rendered him a quadriplegic. The night of Stingley's injury, I'd seen the team doctor tap Stingley's knee, looking for a reflex reaction and getting none. I'd feared the worst then, and on the night of Travis's injury, I feared the worst once again.

Sadly, I was right.

This hit close to home. I was a hockey guy, and more to the point, I was a hockey parent. My son, Ryan, had fallen head over heels in love with the sport at the age of three, sitting down to watch a Boston Bruins game and not getting up until it was over.

Soon, we were playing a name game in the car. I would give the first name of a Bruins player, and he would reply with the last name.

"Ray—"

"—Bourque."

"Cam—"

"—Neely."

All the way down to his personal favorite, "Bruce—"

"—Shoebottom."

Ryan enjoyed all sports, but absolutely *loved* hockey. He would go on to captain his high school team, and then in college, co-captain the Wesleyan Cardinals, helping to lead the team to its most successful year in the history of the program. Hockey also helped him get an outstanding education.

But in the immediate aftermath of Travis's injury, I had my doubts. This was every hockey parent's nightmare, an icicle of piercing terror to the heart.

Yes, I could try to tell myself that riding in an automobile was more dangerous than playing hockey, but a part of me rejected that as a rationalization. Nothing in the world was more important to me than my son. Could I allow him to risk such a catastrophic injury, even for something he loved so much?

I found it especially haunting that Ryan looked all too much like Travis. Blond hair. Good looking. A winsome smile.

Way too close to home.

Ryan continued to play, and with gusto, hoping to someday play college hockey himself, but I never felt at peace with the risks until I interviewed Travis for the first of these pieces. The unfettered love Travis still showed for the sport spoke to me.

Of course, so much else that Travis said also spoke to me. That first time in 1997, then again in 1999, and most recently in 2015.

I'm sure it will speak to you, too.

David H. Hendrickson
December 3, 2017

Foreword

I just reread the three stories that David wrote about me over the years. It's obviously interesting to think back and be reminded of where my life was at during the different time periods and how I felt. I'm surprised at how accurate my memories are of what Dave wrote. There's not much I would say differently today.

I remain brokenhearted to have not ended my hockey career on my own accord, much less just not being able to finish my college career. If I allow myself to think about it, I miss playing hockey as much today as I did when I woke up the day after my accident in the ICU.

I remain frustrated and sad that I don't have a woman in my life to share my highs and lows with. There is still a great deal of sadness, but at the same time I've created a life with the help of my family, friends, and strangers that is far better than I ever expected.

I realize how fortunate I was to spend the first half of my life with a passion, thanks to my hockey career. It took me a while to realize it, but now I feel fortunate to have lived the second half of my life with a purpose. The Travis Roy Foundation was slow to have an impact when it first started out in 1996, but now the foundation has provided significant research grants to top researchers in the country, along with helping roughly 150 people a year live more independently through our adaptive equipment grants program.

I've created a speaking career that has taken me to Canada, Mexico, and throughout the US. I'm no Mike Eruzione, but I've been able to make a living for myself, which has provided me with a sense of confidence. I've gotten to meet a lot of amazing people, many of them being my fellow paralyzed survivors.

It's been upsetting to know of so many additional spinal cord injuries that occurred while playing the game of hockey, whether it be Matt Brown, Jack Jablonski, or more recently Denna Laing, to name a few. I've watched with admiration as they too have figured out their paralyzed lives, but without the assistance of the NCAA catastrophic insurance policy that I benefited from.

The big thing we share in common with our stories is the incredibly loyal and supportive hockey community. I believe I speak for all of us when I say that our lives would be far different had we not had the hockey family behind us.

Last night I was at Agganis Arena to watch the classic Boston University versus Boston College rivalry. I still enjoy watching the game and admire the skills of today's players. I wish I could say that I don't still wonder how my hockey career would've played out.

I will always wonder.

Somebody mentioned to me the other day the saying, "The older I get, the better I was." I feel like I'm drifting into that category as I get older. I wish I had a career full of college and professional statistics so that I knew just where I stood.

I still use many of the same skills and values that the game of hockey taught me. I set my goals and reassess them regularly. Hard work and a positive attitude always seem to pay off.

I also realize how fortunate I am to wake up every day knowing people are rooting for me and for the Travis Roy Foundation. To those of you out there that have been following my story, I remain as grateful as ever for your support.

Travis Roy
December 3, 2017

Introduction to "Travis"

This first story was published on December 3, 1997, fourteen months after Travis's injury. His book, Eleven Seconds: A Story of Tragedy, Courage & Triumph, written with E.M. Swift, had not yet been published, so for some readers, this offered a new glimpse into Travis's life and the challenges of quadriplegia.

It also prompted the first of three exchanges—three feature stories and, I believe, three different editors—who questioned my use of Travis's first name throughout the piece, rather than his last, following the initial use of his full name. This broke the Associated Press usage rule that stipulated that I should have been saying, "Roy this" and "Roy that" instead of "Travis this" and "Travis that."

I didn't care what my well-worn copy of the AP Stylebook said. I wanted to use the fiction writer's *technique of bringing a character closer through use of his first name, rather than distancing with the last name.*

This was "Travis" we were talking about, not "Roy."

I felt a closeness to Travis based on us both being Hockey Guys, and especially based on how forthcoming he'd been about difficult topics. I felt a closeness, and I wanted the readers to feel that closeness, too.

Even if it broke their hearts.

Travis

December 1996

Final exams were over.

Like any other student, Travis Roy felt relief and satisfaction. He'd done well in both of his courses, one in English and one in psychology. Next semester, he'd bump his load up to three courses, and he knew he'd be up to the challenge.

Now, if he were any other student, he'd celebrate and go blow off some steam. Head down to one of the bars that catered to the student crowd and just hang out. Shoot the breeze with friends. Tell lies about the horrors of his first exam week at BU.

Chill out, unwind, meet new people. Laugh at new jokes and old. Let the muscles, tense from final exam pressures, slowly relax. Buy a friend a drink. Let another friend buy him his. The place would be noisy, a loud hum of conversation blanketing the crowd.

If his girlfriend was there, he'd put his arm around her. Hold her close. Look into her eyes. Hug her and, if the time was right, give her a kiss.

And if something wasn't quite right at one place, well, there were plenty more to try. Hop from one to the next.

Shoot pool or play video games. Dance. Mingle. Get a pizza at T. Anthony's. Hop in a car and head downtown, catch a movie, wolf down a medium-rare steak. Go to Chinatown at two in the morning and eat Peking dumplings with chopsticks. Have a snowball fight. Sample the latest CDs at Tower Records.

The social possibilities at a school like BU were endless. And for a hockey player at a school where hockey was king, the sky was the limit.

Exams were over. Ding, dong, the witch is dead. Party hearty, Marty.

But, of course, Travis Roy was not like any other student.

Every academic building was wheelchair accessible, but how many of the popular nightspots were? Hanging out, that simplest of student pleasures, became very different when you were a quadriplegic.

On most days, Travis just shut the door to his room and, with no roommate, shut out the world. He clicked on the TV. Later, he might play on the Internet.

"There were a few people who would come down or call and ask how I was doing or said they'd like to do something with me," he said, "but I always had an excuse. I didn't feel comfortable with myself, and there were very few people who were comfortable with me.

"People don't know all the things that make up a quadriplegic or all the different things that I have to worry about. I don't like putting myself in awkward situations, and I don't like putting other people into them either."

The classroom, that great collegiate melting pot, failed Travis socially even while it met his academic needs. The school, his instructors, and his aides could ensure that he had access to notes and other course materials, but they couldn't alter the discomfort so many felt in his presence.

"You have a group of people that is intimidated by the wheelchair and the handicap itself," he said, "and then you have another group that is intimidated by just Travis Roy, the kid who had been in the news for the past year. Basically, people fell into one of the two groups."

The timing of his injury compounded the social struggles peculiar to any quadriplegic. He'd been little more than six weeks into his first semester at BU. He'd barely known the other players and had yet to forge friendships external to the team.

"When I went to Boston University," he said, "I didn't know anybody. Thus, nobody knew me. I wasn't there long enough to establish myself and have people know me the way I wanted them to know me."

Travis also was struggling to figure out who he was. For so many years, he'd seen himself as A Hockey Player. Now, he was no longer A Hockey Player. A void filled what had once been the core of his self-image.

* * *

Fourteen months earlier, the nightmare had still been a dream. And he had still been A Hockey Player.

"I remember standing there on the blue line," Travis said, "saying to myself, 'This is it. You've made it.' I was so excited. It was a time to enjoy what I'd worked so hard for all my life.

"It was a time of intense pride, for myself and for my family. What I had wanted was to be on that ice, to be part of a Division I hockey team. To be on a Division I hockey team that was the defending national champions just made it that much sweeter."

Then came the fateful first shift. The hop over the dasher, the rush of adrenaline, the head-on crash into the boards and the damaged spinal cord.

"I don't really remember that much of the shift," he said. "It consisted of about eleven seconds, so it was quick. The shift never sunk in, either fortunately or unfortunately; I don't know which would have been better. Before I knew it, it was all over. And I knew it was all over. I knew I wasn't going to be back.... I still remember the hush of the crowd. You could hear a pin drop in that place."

His father, a former star at the University of Vermont, came onto the ice. He reached back to his days as Travis's coach and uttered an almost mantra-like encouragement. "Hey, boy, let's get going. There's a hockey game to play."

"Dad, I'm in deep [trouble]," Travis said.

He couldn't feel his arms, legs, or anything below the pain he felt in his neck. He didn't need a doctor to spell it out for him. He knew.

He had worked so hard, for so many years, to reach this dream that had now turned nightmare. Skating since he was just twenty months old, the son of a rink manager, always looking for a little more ice time…stick boy for a minor league team, soaking up knowledge about the game…leaving his home in Maine to attend prep school where he could play against stronger competition…moving to Boston this past summer so he could work out with Mike Boyle, BU's strength and conditioning coach, and be primed for this season…all that effort to realize a dream…and now this.

"But Dad, I made it," he said.

As they wheeled him off the ice on a stretcher, he saw his girlfriend, Maija Langeland.

"Don't worry," Travis told her. "I'll be all right."

At the hospital, everyone was remarkably calm.

"It was a weird thing because I wasn't in pain," he said. "I just had a little pain in my neck, and that was it. Other than that, I couldn't feel a thing. I looked completely normal. I was in my uniform. I was talking normal[ly]. It was hard to realize how much was gone with that type of injury.

"I remember Maija being there and just wanting to kiss her. She was right by my side. She was as strong as anybody and helped me as much as anybody. She was my rock to hold onto."

In the ensuing weeks, Travis endured surgery, pneumonia, stomach ulcers, high fevers, a partially collapsed lung and a tracheotomy. Unable to speak, first because of tubes down his throat and then because of the tracheotomy, he communicated solely through blinking his eyes, nodding, and an occasional smile.

What became even more difficult, though, was his inability to communicate in the nonverbal ways he'd used all his life: "not being able to hold onto, or hug, or touch, or feel the people who were around me."

Through the ensuing months, those closest to Travis helped him survive emotionally.

"I have an incredible family and an incredible group of friends," he said. "Maija was incredible. That was all I had to get through it. Luckily, that's exactly what I needed."

The team hung his jersey behind the bench for every practice and game. The initials "TR" were added to the Terrier jersey inside a circle above the numerals on the left sleeve.

"It made me feel good that I wasn't forgotten because nobody there really knew me," Travis said. "I was a freshman, and I'd been there a month and a half and that was it. That was the hard part for everybody with the hockey team. Nobody really knew me and knew exactly what kind of person I was. But still they didn't forget me and tried to keep me a part of the team as much as they could.

"It was bittersweet. It felt great not to be forgotten, but to watch the games and see your dream unfolding without you… basically, it went from dream to nightmare in eleven seconds.

"I watched all their games. I didn't live my dream long enough to know exactly what it was all about, so I didn't know what I was missing out on, missing out on traveling and being out on the road and pre-game meals and the atmosphere after a big win or a loss. I only sort of know what my dream was all about."

Five months after the injury, Travis attended his first game when BU went to the NCAA East Regional in Albany, New York. The experience transcended the many games he'd watched on TV.

"It was exciting to see hockey again," he said. "College hockey is just a great game. But it was definitely different. I went down to the locker room before the game and hung out with the guys.

"I remember seeing everyone relate to one another. The freshmen were no longer freshmen. Everybody got along, and everyone had their rituals and buddies on the team.

"It was hard to see all that and not be part of it. It was hard for them because they all wanted to do something for me and say something, but they were at a loss most of the time, much like myself.

"I felt I had a new puzzle, and I didn't know how it went together. I was trying to figure everything out, my relationship with the players and the coach. It was just a tough time."

In September, Travis returned to BU. He had important decisions to make. So much had been left unresolved after his visit to Albany.

"I went down to the rink with Coach Parker," he said. "It was the first time I'd been down there since my accident. And that was when I figured things out. I hadn't known if I was going to go into the rink that day and walk out, close the door, and never go back again or if I wanted to be a part of it.

"I found that I definitely wanted to be a part of it. I love the game too much. It's just an amazing, amazing sport. I couldn't walk away from that."

And so, when the team began practices, he arranged for his van to drive him to Walter Brown Arena every day. His wheelchair might prevent him from taking the ice, but he would once again become an active teammate in his own way. Unfortunately, the blur of a student-athlete's life claimed his plan as a victim.

"I wanted to be there so I could feel more a part of the team," he said. "But I'd forgotten how much time and dedication it takes to be a Division I athlete. It's basically two full-time jobs. They didn't really have that much time to hang out in the locker room. There are so many things going on.

"I'd get down there a half-hour before the practice. They'd get dressed and get out on the ice, and I'd talk a little bit. Then after practice, they would get undressed pretty quick and shower and get to the weight room or the study hall or get doing some homework.

"After a while, I realized that it wasn't a waste of time, but it really wasn't worth me going down there for practice every day.

"And to be honest, we don't have a very deep relationship. I never got to know the guys that well. I'd go down, and we'd talk for a few minutes, but we don't have a whole lot to talk about. I'm not doing the same things they're doing.

"It took a little while for me to figure that out and to realize that I'm not going to be with these guys all the time, hanging out and spending all the time that they spend with each other. There are two separate dreams and two separate goals. I don't think either of us can really appreciate the other's."

Eventually, through trial and error, Travis found a more limited role that fit both his needs and the team's. Although attending practices and pre-game meals amounted to considerable effort with little to show for it, his locker room presence at games benefited everyone and established his place on the team.

For all the home games, and some of those on the road, Travis would be in the locker room, before and after the game and during the intermissions. He'd position himself so he could both see everybody on their way out and also keep his wheelchair out of the way. He'd then move to his game-time position near the arena entrance where he analyzed the action.

"One of my objectives was to try to learn the game from a coaching viewpoint," he said.

Unlike fans who are convinced they could direct strategy better than their coach, Travis found it more difficult than he had expected.

"I struggled with that quite a bit. Jack Parker is an amazing coach. He sees the game so clearly. For me to go up and watch the game and try to figure out forechecks and backchecks and neutral zones was extremely difficult.

"I'd go down to the locker room, and Jack had it all in his mind. He knew exactly what changes needed to be made. It was interesting that way, going down there between periods.

"By hanging out as a player and coming down sort of as a coach between periods, I mixed a whole bunch of things up and made that into my role. I had my place in the locker room and was supportive of the guys. I felt I belonged there, which felt good. I felt the guys liked having me there."

With hockey players a traditionally superstitious lot, some developed locker room rituals involving Travis.

"There were several guys who would come over to me as they went out of the locker room," he said. "I can move my right arm a little bit, and I'd tap my hand to their glove. There are a couple guys that I'd say my few words to every time, and that's what felt good.

"It was all I needed, just to feel that little bit of a part of it and of the guys. It means a lot, it really does, for them to accept me and not only that but accept me the way I wanted to be accepted as a regular kid."

Having finally established his role on the team, Travis tried to put together the rest of the frustrating puzzle of his post-injury life. His family and long-time friends, his girlfriend, Maija, and his newfound place on the team combined to piece together the puzzle's outside border.

What remained, though, were the inside pieces of himself, all looking alike but none of them seeming to fit.

"Hockey was a big part of the pride that I had in myself," he said. "It gave me my confidence in myself. Without it, I don't have much confidence.

"I'm not a hockey player, and after being a hockey player for eighteen years and associating my life as a player, it's quite a difference. I struggle with myself. I haven't figured out my personality as a quadriplegic."

* * *

Summer 1997

When Travis sustained his injury, he and Maija had been going out for a year. In the next year and a half, she would be his "rock" through maddening frustrations and disappointments.

"It obviously has its ups and downs," she would say, "but as time goes by there are more ups than downs. It's definitely do-able."

She stood by Travis's side with the patience and loyalty of a saint.

Not surprisingly, Travis exuded praise.

"Oh, gosh," he said, "she's been the biggest help to me out of anybody since the accident. She supports me in everything I do. We've been able to find a nice balance with our relationship and we're working that all out. Everything is brand new to me again and it's one day at a time, but we have a wonderful relationship."

As summer beckoned, however, Travis and Maija realized that after two and a half years, they needed a break. The two had discussed that eventual possibility even before he headed to BU. If they took a break and it was meant to work out, they told each other, it would work out. Travis's injury, though, both complicated and heightened that need.

"It's taken so much away from her, and her freedom, and her family and her friends," he said. "She needed a break to experience life on her own a little bit. Not only that, but also not to have to worry about all the concerns that I have to worry about every day.

"She just needed to be on her own. We both saw it. I don't know what would have happened without the injury, but the strain of everything definitely contributed to it.

"It's not as much the injury as my personality since the injury. I've really struggled to find myself again. I know who I am and the person that I was before the injury is still inside me and that's the way I think, but I can't physically act in that manner.

"It's amazing how much reflects on not having that. Not being able to do things or show people how much I love them or just to be able to surprise people or do things for them. I can't do that unless I have someone with me.

"The wheelchair has absolutely nothing to do with it. I feel very confident that Maija has no problem with me being a quadriplegic or being in a wheelchair, but my personality is not the same and that's the really frustrating part. I'm trying to figure out how I can be more and more myself in the condition that I am."

* * *

"In a groundbreaking experiment, California scientists have used gene therapy to induce nerves to regrow in rats with damaged spinal cords, partly restoring their ability to walk.... The results are another in a series of recent hopeful steps toward the goal of reversing paralysis from spinal cord injuries."

– The Boston Globe, *page 1*
July 15, 1997

* * *

While presently trying to find himself as a quadriplegic, Travis also looks to a future where spinal cord research offers him the chance to discard his wheelchair.

"I have strong hope, almost to the point where I believe positively, that there will be a cure," he said. "I try and be careful not to set myself up for a big fall, but to be realistic I think there's a very good chance of it happening. The technology these days is moving very rapidly and they are finding big things. It's just a matter of time."

In the meantime, he struggles with himself. The high school athlete with clearly defined goals looks at his life now and can't find any.

"Not right now, to be honest," he said. "That's one of the biggest things I'm dealing with. That's what's most frustrating. I don't have goals and I don't know where to begin.

"It's extremely difficult just trying to figure out what's going to make me happy again. I haven't been able to figure it out.

"I hate to put my life on hold for seven or ten years or however long it will be before they cure it, but right now that's what I'm doing until I figure something out."

Despite the injury's catastrophic effect on his life, though, Travis maintains an abiding love for the sport.

"Any kids I talk to," he said, "I ask them, 'Do you worry about hurting yourself and ending up like me? If you do, don't worry about it. Go out and have fun.'

"I don't even think about hockey being a dangerous sport. That's the most ridiculous thing. It's an amazing, wonderful, wonderful sport. Hopefully, I can give my kids the opportunity to play hockey."

Hear, hear.

Introduction to "The Final 24"

*T*his second story was published almost two years later, on October 30, 1999. Boston University was retiring Travis's number, an event that begged for an update on his life.

I'd seen Travis a few times on the BU campus (primarily in the College of Arts and Sciences building) and we'd always smiled and said hello to each other, sometimes sharing a few more words before we headed to our intended destinations.

This second interview, though, involved a lot more than idle chitchat. Once again, he opened up about the poignant struggles of a young man trying to cope with a life far different than what he had planned.

The Final Number 24

In an ideal world, the ceremony would have been to commemorate Travis Roy's All-America plaque joining the pantheon of BU greats at the entrance to Walter Brown Arena.

In an ideal world, the extended ovation and chants of "Travis! Travis! Travis!" would have brought only smiles and not a pungent mixture of smiles and salty tears. And in an ideal world, Travis Roy would have acknowledged the cheers with a wave of his hand, hugged his father, mother, and sister, and then taken his seat, knowing that later he could walk out of the arena and down to T. Anthony's or T's Pub.

But it isn't always an ideal world. And life sometimes is very bleeping unfair. Sometimes the true heroes have to shoot for sights a good deal lower than what they originally expected.

On this evening, Boston University celebrated just such a hero, retiring Travis Roy's jersey and, with it, the number 24. A banner now hangs from Walter Brown Arena signifying the first number the hockey program has ever retired.

"It was awesome," said Travis. "I've really wanted to turn the page. There have been a lot of sad times, but this is a happy moment. Now it's time to turn the page and be proud of everything that has gone on here.

"I love this place. I love BU hockey. I love Coach [Jack] Parker. I couldn't be surrounded by a better group of people…. They're amazing…and wonderful people.

"They have no idea how it's been for them to continue to support me and to acknowledge me and just be so kind in everything they do. It's a cliché, but you just can't say enough. It's a wonderful area we live in and people should be proud of what they've done and how they've handled me."

After losing his original freshman year to the rehabilitation that followed his spinal cord injury, Travis has maintained a pace of studies that will see him graduate this year with a degree in Communications and Public Relations.

"My first freshman year was a wipeout, but since then I've done it in four years," he said. "I'm awfully proud of that.

"I'm one to set goals and I'm one to accomplish goals. That goal was set early on [so] I guess it doesn't surprise me that I pulled that one off."

It's an accomplishment that understandably fills his parents with great pride.

"It would have been real easy to pack it in in his situation or anybody who is faced with this kind of physical setback," said Lee Roy, Travis's father. "Just pack your bag and head on home.

"He hasn't been home in a long time," said Lee Roy with a laugh, "and that's great. He's doing very well down here.

"There's a great deal of pride, obviously, but there's the disappointment that Travis didn't have the chance to do what he wanted to do on the ice. Obviously, for Jack Parker and the rest of the Boston University community to honor Travis in this way…it couldn't be any better. But at the same time it's very bittersweet.

"For me, the heartbreak is that the record book will show that Travis played one game with a 0-0-0 [scoring line]. Over the past four years, there were the hopes that somehow, someway he wouldn't be remembered as a player who played one game.

"But there's a lot of pride in what he's been able to accomplish, to have over a 3.0 average, make the Dean's List last semester and to graduate in four years when you discount the one year of rehab. I'm so very proud of what he's done and the way that he's done it."

Since his injury, Travis has become a tremendous source of inspiration to others who have suffered a similar fate.

"In some ways I've been put in that role," he said. "I've always enjoying being in a leadership role. I always cherished being captain of the teams that I was on.

"It's certainly a different team that I'm leading now. But if I can be inspirational and put a positive spin on people in wheelchairs and paralysis, I [might even] help out my own cause and hopefully get out of this chair someday."

Travis is still taking a wait-and-see approach as to what the future holds for him after graduation. But it doesn't necessarily include hockey.

"I still love the sport," he said. "It was a fluke accident. But there's definitely some sadness. I'm just trying to figure out a way to enjoy it. I don't think I'll ever enjoy it as much as I did when I was playing the sport, but I guess I'm looking for the next best thing.

"I don't know what's going to happen. Getting away [from hockey] for a little bit, basically I'm trying to open as many doors as I can and see what's out there and see what I'd like to do.

"I'd like to be one of those few people who wake up nowadays and feels passionate about their job and can't wait to get to it. I've just got to figure out what it's going to be."

In the meantime, he's taking one day at a time.

"I live on a lot of clichés that you hear every day, but they work," he said. "So it's one day at a time and you just try to keep a smile on your face.

"I'm doing my best. There are the ups and downs still, but there are a lot more ups [now]. I still have my struggles, but school is going well and I'll be graduating in May.

"I've got a long life ahead of me and I'm really looking forward to it."

Introduction to "Travis, Twenty Years Later"

I *cringe when the word "anniversary" is used in reference to tragedies. The dictionary allows the word to be used for memorable events both good and bad, but for me, the word instinctively feels best associated with celebrations.*

So I never used the word "anniversary" as the twenty-year mark from Travis's injury approached. But I knew it was time to talk to Travis again. Once again, he freely spoke of his life, even when we ventured into the most heartbreaking of personal challenges.

Travis,
Twenty Years Later

October 20, 2015

O n October 20, 1995, Travis Roy's collegiate hockey career ended almost before it started. Just eleven seconds into his first shift for Boston University, he crashed headfirst into the boards while trying to deliver a check, cracking his fourth vertebra and damaging his spinal cord.

In an instant, his dream-come-true became a nightmare.

His life as a hockey player ended abruptly; his life as a quadriplegic began.

Now, twenty years later, so much has changed from his life before that fateful shift, yet a few constants remain.

"I think about hockey every day," he says. "It goes through my mind regularly."

And at night, he still, on occasion, dreams the same dreams of many hockey players: his big chance has arrived but he can't find his stick, he didn't pack his gloves, or his skates are broken.

"In the dreams, I'm always letting [former Boston University] coach [Jack] Parker down because I'm not ready to go," Travis says. "I wake up with the emotions and have to tell myself that it was just a dream and I haven't let Coach down yet."

In his role as a motivational speaker, he even shows a video of the accident as part of his presentation.

"I'm pretty numb to it now," he says, "but I keep hoping the video ends up differently."

The video, of course, never changes. The reality of quadriplegia remains. As does the love for the sport, but it's a love now tinged with great sadness.

"I still enjoy hockey," Travis says. "I'm still amazed by the sport, I really am, by the speed and the grace. It's such a special, special sport.

"[But] I am brokenhearted over hockey. It was my first love.

"I didn't expect it to go away, but I can still feel it, I can still smell it. I just love it. I love it."

The Boston Bruins recently signed Travis to a one-day

contract and had him drop the ceremonial first puck while wearing a Bruins jersey with his name and BU number, 24, on the back. It was a heartwarming honor, but a bittersweet one when considering what might have been.

"There was a little piece of it being a dream come true," he says. "It just wasn't the way I'd planned it at all. I still wish I had the other opportunity, too. I still wish I could have traveled the other road.

"I'll never know what kind of player I was going to turn out to be. But when I look at the guys who made it [in the NHL], they had something special. In my gut, I think I would have made it."

Instead, paralysis imposed severe limitations on a life that had appeared to have a limitless future. Those limitations remain to this day.

"As far as taking care of myself and getting up and ready for the day, I can't do anything," Travis says. "I'm so limited.

"Once I'm in my wheelchair, once I'm set up for the day and I can get over to my computer and I've got my earpiece in my ear for my phone, that's when my independence grows. The computer and technology is my world, and it has enabled me to do so much of what I've done for the last twenty years."

What has made the biggest difference is that Boston University was part of the NCAA's catastrophic insurance policy. As a result, Travis's long-term, around-the-clock care is covered, which is far from the norm for quadriplegics.

"I do have twenty-four seven home care year-round," he says. "So I can do what I want and when I want with the help of that care. That's been a major relief.

"It's not my mom and my dad that's getting me up and ready for the day or my sister or my friends. That's what most people with this condition have to deal with. It becomes very [overwhelming] for family and friends.

"And if it's not family and friends doing it, it's limited hours [of care] through the state and Medicare and Medicaid. Home care is not a pretty business, quite frankly."

Conspicuous by its absence in Travis's list of his possible aid-givers is that of a girlfriend or wife. In the immediate aftermath of the injury, his girlfriend at the time, Maija Langeland, remained a rock by his side. Eventually, though, they went their separate ways.

Romantic relationships have remained difficult, if not quite impossible, ever since. In many ways, it's one of the cruelest things taken from so many quadriplegics.

"I've only had a couple relationships since my injury," Travis says. "I had one shortly after it, a master's student doing physical therapy. She was great and a beautiful girl.

"But it was too frustrating for me. I was the one that brought it to an end."

Travis didn't try again until about a year ago.

"I figured after all these years I'd give it a shot," he says. "I was older and wiser and at a different stage in my life. But after a month I found myself in the exact same place. It was so frustrating. I ended that relationship as well.

"It's a missing piece [in my life]. I kind of hoped to have kids. I kind of hoped to have a wife. But I can't be the person that I want to be, and I can't pretend otherwise.

"It's really hard. It's another devastating, frustrating piece of paralysis. Being a quadriplegic in a relationship takes a lot of your masculinity away.

"I miss the passion. I miss the romance. I miss the friendship. I miss the partnership. I miss everything that comes with a relationship."

Although almost all of that sadness can be laid at the cruel feet of quadriplegia, Travis takes some of the blame.

"It doesn't have to be that way," he says. "Part of it is me, it's very much me.

"I know people who have figured it out and found love in a relationship. But for me, I'm a little stubborn. I can't pretend. I can't be the person that I am inside. The person inside can't express himself the way I want to through daily physical activities, whether it's opening a door or [lying] on the couch and cuddling or any of that."

Although nothing can come close to making up for all that Travis lost, he can still look at some things he's gained.

"The older I get, the wiser I am," he says, now forty years old. "I've learned a lot of lessons at a very early age."

One of the most important ones was reiterated in a TED Talk he recently watched, one with the message that if you want to be happy, be grateful.

"I'm not the happiest person in the world, but considering my circumstances I'm a pretty happy person," Travis says. "I am grateful. I'm at a point where I look around at my friends, some family members and peers, and I'm a lot happier than these people are.

"Why is that? Not only because I love and really appreciate my family, but I actually take the time and call them and I do things with them and I acknowledge those moments. Brand names and money, faster cars and bigger homes, you can have them. Give me a nice home and a warm bed and no major financial burdens or worries, and that'll make me a happy guy.

"I have to sit and watch a lot. I watch people interact. I sit on the sidelines in a lot of ways. You learn a lot about people when you watch and listen.

"The biggest lesson is that life is simple, a lot more simple than people realize. You just have to cut out all the noise and figure out what are the two or three or four things that are really important to you. Then [evaluate] how much time, energy, and focus you're putting into those things and integrating them into your day and your life. That's what I've learned and that's what I do."

Aside from friends and family, Travis has chosen to put most of his energies into his foundation, The Travis Roy Foundation, which is dedicated to enhancing the lives of individuals with spinal cord injuries and their families. Recently, it has increased fundraising to about $1 million per year, which is then spent half on research and half on grants to individuals ranging from $1,000 to $7,000.

"It's a huge part of who I am and what I do and what I spend my time on," Travis says. "To touch all those lives is a special opportunity.

"Paralysis is a really horrible thing, especially quadriplegia. With paraplegia, people can still be pretty independent and live a really productive life, but if you're a quadriplegic, the amount of energy that goes into your care can be pretty exhausting. I haven't given up on research; I want to see paralysis come to an end."

That burning desire goes far beyond whatever personal improvement he might achieve.

"I don't know how much I'm going to benefit from the research at this point," he says. "I'm twenty years in and I don't know if I'm going to walk. I'd be very grateful, just for the sake of my independence, to get [use of] my arms and my fingers and not need twenty-four seven home care.

"At this point, hopefully, that's a realistic goal. I don't know if I'm going to walk, but if you let me live by myself independently, that would be huge.

"There are too many young people in nursing homes because there's no one to care for them and the families can't handle it. There are problems with infections, pressure sores, and complications of the bowels and bladder. Nobody wants to talk about this topic because it's not fun to talk about.

"Paralysis is devastating. You can live with it, it's bearable, and you can live a very productive and successful life, and that's what I'm doing. But I'm doing it with some financial resources, backed by the money that was raised for me, with great insurance, with family, friends, and with a unique opportunity to have a career speaking and making a living. Most people with my problem don't have that.

"I want the next generation, my niece and nephews, not to have to see their friends go through this. I want to be a part of putting an end to paralysis."

Helping Others Move Forward

The Travis Roy Foundation is dedicated to enhancing the life of individuals with spinal cord injuries and their families.

HELPING OTHERS

Half of the money raised by the Travis Roy Foundation goes toward Quality of Life Grants to purchase adaptive equipment.

Grants

At the Travis Roy Foundation we are focused on empowering spinal cord injured survivors through adaptive equipment grants, which enable independence;

and funding SCI research to benefit people with chronic injuries. In doing this we actively collaborate with the SCI community to create advocacy and to raise awareness.

Examples of eligible items include upgrade and maintenance of wheelchairs, vehicle modifications (i.e., hand controls or lifts), small home modifications including ramp and lift installation, computers, and other adaptive equipment.

FINDING A CURE

The Travis Roy Foundation has awarded over two million dollars in research grants towards finding a cure.

SCI Research

The Travis Roy Foundation is dedicated to improving the lives of those with spinal cord injuries. The Foundation recognizes the importance of funding research to discover therapies and methods to treat spinal cord injuries that are recent or acute, but also understands the importance of funding studies that will help improve the quality of life of people who have been living with spinal cord injuries for years.

PARTICIPATE

There are many ways you can get directly involved with the Travis Roy Foundatation. Show your support today!

Get Involved

There are many ways to get involved with the Travis Roy Foundation.

Go to https://www.travisroyfoundation.org to see how you can help.

Donations

Please consider donating to the Travis Roy Foundation to fund research and also help those who are victims of spinal cord injuries. Contact the foundation:

Travis Roy Foundation
Hemenway & Barnes LLP
101 Huntington Avenue, Suite 520
Boston, MA 02199
Email: info@travisroyfoundation.org